Adventures

THE SHAPE OF POETRY

How do you like to go up in a swing,
Up in the air so blue?
Oh, I do think it the pleasantest thing
Ever a child can do!

—Robert Louis Stevenson

illustrated by Gwen Connelly

THE CHILD'S WORLD

ELGIN, ILLINOIS 60120

compiled by Diane Dow Suire

Distributed by Childrens Press, 1224 West Van Buren Street, Chicago, Illinois 60607.

Library of Congress Cataloging in Publication Data

Main entry under title:

Adventures.

(The Shape of poetry)
Summary: A collection of poems about play and imaginary adventures by American and English authors including Robert Louis Stevenson, Dorothy Aldis, and Rachel Field.
1. Children's poetry, American.   2. Children's poetry, English.   [1. American poetry—Collections.
2. English poetry—Collections.   3. Play—Poetry.
4. Imagination—Poetry]   I. Series.   II. Connelly, Gwen, ill.
PS586.3.A38   1984   811'.008-09282   83-25212
ISBN 0-89565-265-X

1 2 3 4 5 6 7 8 9 10 11 12 R 91 90 89 88 87 86 85 84

Adventures

5003446

My BED is like a little boat;
   Mom helps me in when I embark.
She dresses me in my sailor's coat
   And starts me in the dark.

At night, I go on board and say
   Good-night to all my friends on shore.
I shut my eyes and sail away
   And see and hear no more.

And sometimes things to bed I take,
   As wise sailors have to do—
Perhaps a slice of birthday cake,
   Perhaps a toy or two.

All night across the dark we steer;
   But when the day returns at last,
Safe in my room, beside the pier,
   I find my vessel fast.

—Robert Louis Stevenson

I'M HIDING, I'm hiding,
  And no one knows where;
For all they can see are my
  Toes and my hair.

And I just heard my father
  Say to my mother—
"But, darling, he must be
  Somewhere or other.

"Have you looked in the inkwell?"
  And Mother said, "Where?"
"In the inkwell," said Father. But
  I was not there.

Then "Wait!" cried my mother—
  "I think that I see
Him under the carpet." But
  It was not me.

"Inside the mirror's
    A pretty good place,"
Said Father and looked, but saw
    Only his face.

"We've hunted," sighed Mother,
    "As hard as we could;
And I am so afraid that we've
    Lost him for good."

Then I laughed out loud,
    And I wiggled my toes;
And Father said—"Look, dear,
    I wonder if those

"Toes could be Benny's?
    There are ten of them, see?"
And they *were* so surprised to find
    Out it was me!

—Dorothy Aldis

I OFTEN sit and wish that I
Could be a kite up in the sky,
And ride upon the breeze and go
Whichever way I chanced to blow.

—*Anonymous*

WHEN my brother Tommy
Sleeps in bed with me,
   He doubles up
   And makes
      himself
      exactly
         like
            a
               V.
And 'cause the bed is not so wide,
A part of him is on my side.

— A. B. Ross

HOW do you like to go up in a swing,
  Up in the air so blue?
Oh, I do think it the pleasantest thing
  Ever a child can do!

Up in the air and over the wall,
  Till I can see so wide,
Rivers and trees and cattle and all
  Over the countryside—

Till I look down on the garden green,
  Down on the roof so brown—
Up in the air I go flying again,
  Up in the air and down!

—Robert Louis Stevenson

WHEN at home alone I sit,
And am very tired of it,
I have just to shut my eyes
To go sailing through the skies—
To go sailing far away
To the pleasant Land of Play.

—*Robert Louis Stevenson*

I AM the sister of him
And he is my brother.
He is too little for us
To talk to each other.

So every morning I show him
My doll and my book;
But every morning he still is
Too little to look.

—Dorothy Aldis

ANIMAL crackers, and cocoa to drink,
That is the finest of suppers, I think;
When I'm grown up and can have what I please,
I think I shall always insist upon these.

What do *you* choose when you're offered a treat?
When Mother says, "What would you like best to eat?"
Is it waffles and syrup, or cinnamon toast?
It's cocoa and animals that *I* love the most!

—Christopher Morley

PURPLE horses with orange manes,
Elephants pink and blue,
Tigers and lions that never were seen
In a circus parade or zoo!
Bring out your money and choose your steed,
And prance to delightsome sound.
What fun if the world would turn some day
Into a Merry-Go-Round!

— Rachel Field

THE WOODS are full of fairies!
   The trees are all alive:
The river overflows with them,
   See how they dip and dive!

What funny little fellows!
   What dainty little dears!
They dance and leap, and prance and peep,
   And utter fairy cheers!

I'd like to tame a fairy,
   To keep it on a shelf,
To see it wash its little face,
   And dress its little self.

— Anonymous

17

THE ATTIC window's in the ceiling;
　　You only see the clouds go by;
And when I'm there I have a feeling
　　Of being very near the sky.

The attic air is warm and dusty,
　　And there are boxes full of things,
And rods of iron, rather rusty,
　　And beds and trunks and curtain rings.

I often like to go and play there;
　　I take my storybook and toys;
It seems so very far away there,
　　From all the people and the noise.

But when the blue behind the skylight
　　Has faded to a dingy grey,
And a mouse scrabbles in the twilight,
　　I leave my things and go away.

—Rose Fyleman

I HAD a little tea-party,
  This afternoon at three;
    'Twas very small,
      Three guests in all,
Just I, myself, and me.

Myself ate up the sandwiches,
  While I drank up the tea,
    'Twas also I
      Who ate the pie
And passed the cake to me.

—*Jessica Nelson North*

WE BROUGHT a rug for sitting on,
Our lunch was in a box.
The sand was warm. We didn't wear
Hats or shoes or socks.
Waves came curling up the beach.
We waded. It was fun.
Our sandwiches were different kinds.
I dropped my jelly one.

—Dorothy Aldis

AFTER my bath
I try, try, try
to wipe myself
till I'm dry, dry, dry.

Hands to wipe
fingers and toes
and two wet legs
and a shiny nose.

Just think how much
less time I'd take
if I were a dog
and could shake, shake, shake.

—Aileen Fisher

IF I HAD a hundred dollars to spend,
  Or maybe a little more,
I'd hurry as fast as my legs would go
  Straight to the animal store.

I wouldn't say, "How much for this or that?"
  "What kind of dog is he?"
I'd buy as many as rolled an eye,
  Or wagged a tail at me!

I'd take the hound with the drooping ears
  That sits by himself alone;
Cockers and Cairns and wobbly pups
  For to be my very own.

I might buy a parrot all red and green,
  And the monkey I saw before,
If I had a hundred dollars to spend,
  Or maybe a little more.

—Rachel Field

JUMP—jump—jump—
  Jump away
From this town into
  The next, today.

Jump—jump—jump—
  Jump over the moon;
Jump all the morning
And all the noon.

Jump—jump—jump—
  Jump all night;
Won't our mothers
  Be in a fright?

Jump—jump—jump—
  Over the sea;
What wonderful wonders
  We shall see.

Jump—jump—jump—
  Jump far away;
And all come home
  Some other day.

—Kate Greenaway

WHEN I was sick and lay a-bed,
I had two pillows at my head,
And all my toys beside me lay
To keep me happy all the day.

And sometimes for an hour or so
I watched my leaden soldiers go,
With different uniforms and drills,
Among the bed-clothes, through the hills.

And sometimes sent my ships in fleets
All up and down among the sheets;
Or brought my trees and houses out,
And planted cities all about.

I was the giant great and still
That sits upon the pillow-hill,
And sees before him, dale and plain,
The pleasant land of counterpane.

—Robert Louis Stevenson

HALFWAY down the stairs
Is a stair
Where I sit.
There isn't any
Other stair
Quite like
It.
I'm not at the bottom,
I'm not at the top;
So this is the stair
Where
I always
Stop.

Halfway up the stairs
Isn't up,
And isn't down.
It isn't in the nursery,
It isn't in the town.
And all sorts of funny thoughts
Run around my head:
"It isn't really
Anywhere!
It's somewhere else
Instead!"

—A. A. Milne

Grateful acknowledgement is made to the following for permission to reprint their copyrighted material.

"Hiding" (pg. 6), "Little" (pg. 13), and "Picnic" (pg. 21) reprinted by permission of Putnam Publishing Group from ALL TOGETHER by Dorothy Aldis. Copyright 1952 by Dorothy Aldis, copyright renewed 1980 by Roy E. Porter.

"Two In Bed" (pg. 9) from FIVE GOING ON SIX by A. B. Ross. All rights reserved. Reprinted by permission of Holt, Rinehart and Winston, Publishers.

"Animal Crackers" (p. 14) from CHIMNEYSMOKE by Christopher Morley. (J. B. Lippincott) Poem copyright 1917, 1945, by Christopher Morley. By permission of Harper & Row, Publishers, Inc.

"Merry-Go-Round" (p. 16) by Rachel Field from THE POINTED PEOPLE. Reprinted with permission of Macmillan Publishing Company. (New York: Macmillan, 1957)

"The Attic" (pg. 19) from FAIRIES AND FRIENDS by Rose Fyleman. Reprinted by permission of The Society of Authors.

"Three Guests" (pg. 20) by Jessica Nelson North, reprinted by permission of the author.

"After a Bath" (pg. 22) by Aileen Fisher, reprinted by permission of the author.

"The Animal Store" (pg. 24) from Taxis and Toadstools by Rachel Field. Copyright 1926 by Doubleday & Company, Inc. Reprinted by permission of the publisher. Copyright © 1924 by Yale Publishing Company. Copyright © 1926 by Crowell Publishing Company. First published in GB 1962.

"Halfway Down" (pg. 30) from WHEN WE WERE VERY YOUNG by A. A. Milne, copyright 1924 by E. P. Dutton & Co., Inc.; copyright renewed 1952 by A. A. Milne. Reprinted by permission of E. P. Dutton; The Canadian Publishers, McClellan and Stewart Limited, Toronto; and Methuen Children's Books.